CELEBRATING
ADVENT
IN THE
SANCTUARY

Ralph Dessem

CELEBRATING ADVENT IN THE SANCTUARY

0384 / ISBN 0-89536-635-5

PRINTED IN U.S.A.

Dedicated To
Larry, Dean, Mark
and Carol
who have all had the opportunity
to light the Advent candles in
the sanctuary

THE ADVENT SEASON

The Advent season has a long tradition in the history of the Christian Church, beginning somewhere near the end of the fourth century. While it was originally celebrated for a period of forty days and included fasting, by the beginning of the seventh century it was confined to the four-week period preceding Christmas. In the calendar of the Christian Church today, the season begins on the Sunday nearest to St. Andrew's Day (Nov. 30th) and includes the four Sundays preceding Christmas as well as the intervening weekdays. It is the first of the six seasons of the Christian Year.

While Advent, in the past, has been observed in many churches as a time of penitence in preparation for the joyous celebration of Christmas, the emphasis has changed recently to one of anticipation. It calls to mind the four-thousand years of waiting for the coming of the Messiah on the part of the Hebrew people. In many churches today, there is also an emphasis upon the second coming of our Lord. For the Christian, Advent not only becomes a time of preparation for the celebration of the coming of Christ into the world, but also a time for the rebirth of his spirit in our lives.

THE COLORS OF ADVENT

With this changing emphasis of Advent has also come a change in the color of the season. While purple has been the traditional color for many years, this symbolizes penitence and such is not the emphasis in many churches. The color has changed to royal blue, symbolizing the sense of expectation. It is designed to call forth anticipation in our hearts — hopeful waiting for the celebration of Christmas once again and for the second coming of our Lord. This new color of Advent also serves to distinguish the season from Lent in our Church Year.

The color of the Advent season in the church sanctuary is gradually changing from purple to royal blue. This new color is now available in ministerial stoles and paraments. Many churches are adding the royal blue paraments to the sets they once thought were complete. Likewise, the candles of the Advent wreath are now appearing in blue as well as purple.

PREPARING THE SANCTUARY

The church sanctuary ought to be changed prior to the first Sunday of Advent so that each worshiper will know something is different when he first enters. It ought to remind everyone present that the new Church Year is beginning and help the congregation share in the expectation of the season. Of course, the change in the color of the paraments will be the first evidence of Advent seen by those who come for worship.

The Jesse Tree, placed in the chancel or at some significant location, will call to mind the Old Testament promises of the coming of the Messiah. This symbolic tree is named after Jesse, the father of David, and reminds us that Jesus was of the lineage of David. It usually consists of a bare tree on which are hung various symbols of Old Testament prophecy. In some churches such symbols are made by the children in Church School classes and then placed on the tree in a ceremony on the first Sunday of Advent. The Jesse Tree should be removed from the sanctuary before Christmas Eve and replaced by a Christmas tree or a Chrismon tree.

Banners hung at an appropriate spot in the sanctuary can help remind the congregation of the meaning of the season. Rather than hanging them all prior to the first Sunday in Advent, begin with one and add another each week. It will be more meaningful if the banners follow a certain theme or contain works which are appropriate to the season: HOPE — FAITH — JOY — LOVE.

Of course, the significance of the Advent season can probably be portrayed best through the lighting of a large Advent wreath on each of the four Sundays. (Described in detail later in this booklet.)

THE HYMNS OF ADVENT

Certain hymns are most appropriate for use in the worship services during this season. Those used will vary according to denomination and local church custom.

Here are some suggested hymns found in the hymnals of the major denominations:

Name	Tune
O Come, O Come, Emmanuel	Veni Emmanuel
The King Shall Come	St. Stephen
Break Forth, O Living Light of God	St. Stephen
Of the Father's Love Begotten	Divinum Mysterium
Hail to the Lord's Anointed	Ellacombe or Rockport
Watchman, Tell Us of the Night	Aberystwyth
Come, Thou Long-Expected Jesus	Hyfrydol or Stuttgart
The People That in Darkness Sat	Caithness
There's a Voice in the Wilderness Crying	Hereford
Lift Up Your Heads, Ye Mighty Gates	Truro
The Heavens Declared Thy Glory, Lord	Hebron
The Advent of Our God	Franconia
Wake, Awake, for Night is Flying	Wachet Auf
On Jordan's Bank the Baptist's Cry	Winchester New
Prepare the Way, O Zion	Messiah
The King Shall Come When Morning Dawns	
	Farrant
Lo! He Comes With Clouds Descending	Storl
Comfort, Comfort Ye My People	Psalm 42

THE LECTIONARY TEXTS

The texts of the Unified Lectionary will vary from one year to another in the A, B, and C cycles since each follows a different gospel. However, there is great similarity in the themes of the three years during the Advent season. There is a progression in these themes as they guide the worshiper on his/her Advent pilgrimage.

A general summary of the Advent themes is as follows:

First Sunday in Advent — Expectation
As the Old Testament prophets foretold the coming of the Messiah, so Jesus has told us of his second coming. We should wait in anticipation of his coming as the people of Israel longed for the promised Messiah.

Second Sunday in Advent — Preparation
John the Baptist prepared the way for the coming of the Christ. So must we prepare our lives to receive his spirit anew within us. This calls for repentance on our part just as it did in the days of John the Baptist.

Third Sunday in Advent — Proclamation
We rejoice because his coming is near at hand. Our faith is strengthened as we are reminded that he will come to earth again, as he did many years ago. Our hearts are filled with joy as we proclaim that the realization of his promise is near.

Fourth Sunday in Advent — Revelation
We praise God for the promise about to be fulfilled through him. We thank him for the revelation of his love for humankind through the gift of his Son.

Christmas Eve or Christmas Day — Celebration

The promise of God has now become a reality. The prophecies of long ago have been fulfilled. God has completed his plan for humankind by sending his Son into the world, and we celebrate his coming.

THE LECTIONARY READINGS FOR ADVENT

SERIES A	SERIES B	SERIES C
First Sunday in Advent		
Psalm 122	Psalm 80:1-7	Psalm 25:1-10
Isaiah 2:1-5	Isaiah 63:16-64:4	Jeremiah 33:14-16
Romans 13:11-14	1 Corinthians 1:3-9	1 Thessalonians
Matthew 24:36-44	Mark 13:32-37	3:9-15
		Luke 21:25-36
Second Sunday in Advent		
Psalm 72:1-19	Psalm 85	Psalm 126
Isaiah 11:1-10	Isaiah 40:1-11	Malachi 3:1-4
Romans 15:4-9	2 Peter 3:8-14	Philippians 1:3-11
Matthew 3:1-12	Mark 1:1-8	Luke 3:1-6
Third Sunday in Advent		
Psalm 146	Luke 1:46b-55	Isaiah 12:2-6
Isaiah 35:1-10	Isaiah 61:1-4, 8-11	Zephaniah 3:14-18
James 5:7-10	1 Thessalonians	Philippians 4:4-9
Matthew 11:2-11	5:16-24	Luke 3:7-18
	John 1:6-8, 19-28	
Fourth Sunday in Advent		
Psalm 24	Psalm 89:1-4, 14-18	Psalm 80:1-7
Isaiah 7:10-15	2 Samuel 7:8-16	Micah 5:1-4
Romans 1:1-7	Romans 16:25-27	Hebrews 10:5-10
Matthew 1:18-25	Luke 1:26-38	Luke 1:39-47
Christmas Eve or Christmas Day		
Psalm 96	Psalm 97	Psalm 98
Isaiah 9:2-7	Isaiah 62:6-12	Isaiah 52:6-10
Titus 2:11-15	Colossians 1:15-20	Hebrews 1:1-12
Luke 2:1-20	Matthew 1:18-25	John 1:1-14

THE ADVENT WREATH

The Advent wreath is traced back to an old Scandinavian custom celebrating the coming of light after a season of darkness. The Christian Church has used it to symbolize the coming of Christ as the Light of the World after four-thousand years of darkness. As the Advent candles are lighted, this truth is symbolized anew in the lives of the worshipers. The circle of evergreen reminds us of the promise of eternal life through Jesus Christ.

To make the Advent wreath, one secures the ends of four candles into the circle of evergreen at equal distances from each other. It is best to have a base of wood or styrofoam with holes into which the candles may be fitted. The completed Advent wreath may be placed on a table in the chancel, or it may be suspended from the ceiling. Attractive pedestals may also be purchased for the placing of the wreath.

The candles are usually three purple and one pink, although royal blue is now becoming quite popular. The pink candle is to be lighted on the third Sunday and symbolizes joy. This is based on the Latin word *gaudete* which means *rejoice.* In the ancient tradition of the Church when fasting was observed throughout Advent, Gaudete Sunday was the one day when a break in this custom could be observed. It also symbolized rejoicing because the coming of the Lord was near at hand. In some churches large white candles are used and a small purple ribbon is tied on each one. On Christmas Day these ribbons are changed to red and left until Epiphany.

Regardless of the size of the Advent wreath or the colors of the candles in it, the item of central importance is the Christ candle. This is a large white candle placed in the center of the wreath and lighted on Christmas Eve or Christmas Day.

THE LIGHTING OF THE ADVENT CANDLES

The lighting of the candles in the Advent wreath ought to take place early in the worship service so that the congregation will have as much time as possible to appreciate them and their meaning. The lighting may be done by a specific group of children or youth, rather than by the acolyte. If children are participating, use different ones each Sunday and use several when more than one candle is to be lighted.

The services on the following pages are designed to be used when the candles of the Advent wreath are lighted in the sanctuary. They may be used without requesting specific permission from the publisher.

The Service for the First Sunday in Advent

EXPECTATION

The Opening Words (by leader)
God inspired the prophets of old that they should foretell of his great promise of a Messiah. Many generations of people lived in expectation, hoping that this promise would be fulfilled in their day. We also live in a day of anticipation, knowing that Christ will return to us, perhaps in our lifetime.

The Reading of the Lectionary Text
(Gospel suggested)

The Lighting of the First Advent Candle
(As a purple, or blue candle is lighted, the leader may say:)
Today, as we begin the Advent season, the Candle of Expectation is lighted. May it serve to remind us of God's great promise to humankind, and that he always keeps his promises.

The Hymn: "Come Thou Long Expected Jesus"
(or another one appropriate to the day)

The Prayer (by leader)
Heavenly Father, may we have a new appreciation of your promises to us and your fulfillment of them. Help us to prepare our lives for his advent within us during this holy season. In his name we pray. Amen.

The Service for the Second Sunday in Advent

PREPARATION

The Opening Words (by leader)
John the Baptist prepared the way for Jesus to come into the world. His call to repentance challenged his listeners to consider their relationship with God. They were to repent of their sins and then so discipline their lives that they would be ready to receive him when he came.

The Reading of the Lectionary Text
(Gospel suggested)

The Lighting of the First and Second Advent Candles
(As the first purple, or blue candle is relighted, and a second of the same color lighted, the leader may say:)
Today we relight the Candle of Expectation, reminding us of God's great promise that he would send a Messiah to save his people. As we light the Candle of Preparation, it reminds us that as John the Baptist prepared the way for Jesus, so we also need to prepare ourselves for his coming into our lives.

The Hymn: "On Jordan's Bank the Baptist's Cry"
(or another one appropriate to the day)

The Prayer (by leader)
Dear Lord, guide us in confessing our sinfulness to you. We know that out of the greatness of your love you have promised to forgive us. Cleanse us now as we prepare for the coming of Jesus again; this we ask in his name. Amen.

The Service for the Third Sunday in Advent

PROCLAMATION

The Opening Words (by leader)

The prophets not only proclaimed that God would send his Son into the world, but they also foretold the rejoicing that would accompany his coming. The hearts of men, women and children were filled with joy and gladness as the realization of his promise drew near.

The Reading of the Lectionary Text
(Gospel suggested)

The Lighting of the First, Second, and Third Advent Candles

(As the first and second purple, or blue candles are relighted, and the third (pink) candle is lighted, the leader may say:)

Today we relight the Candle of Expectation, recalling God's promise to send a Savior to his people. As we relight the Candle of Preparation, we remember how John the Baptist prepared the way for Jesus. Now, as we light the Candle of Proclamation, our hearts are filled with joy as we proclaim that his advent will soon take place.

The Hymn: "O Come, O Come, Emmanuel"
("Rejoice! Rejoice! Emmanuel")

The Prayer (by leader)

O God, we rejoice in the advent of your Son and await the day when he will return. May our lives be filled with joy as you guide us in proclaiming his truth to those around us each day; in Christ's name we pray. Amen.

The Service for the Fourth Sunday in Advent

REVELATION

The Opening Words (by leader)
The revelation of God's love for humankind is seen through the gift of his Son on the first Christmas. We have learned what God is like through the life and teachings of Jesus, and we have discovered the true meaning of love through his death on our behalf.

The Reading of the Lectionary Text
(Gospel suggested)

The Lighting of the Four Advent Candles
(As the first three candles are relighted and the fourth candle is lighted, the leader may say:)
Today we relight the Candle of Expectation, recalling God's promise to send a Savior, and the Candle of Preparation, remembering John the Baptist preparing the way for Jesus, and the Candle of Proclamation, reminding us of the joy that comes from telling others of his coming. Now, as we light the Candle of Revelation, our lives are filled with the greatness of his love, revealed through the coming of the Christ-Child.

The Hymn: "Hail to the Lord's Anointed"
(or another one appropriate to the day)

The Prayer (by leader)
Father, we thank you for the manner in which you revealed yourself through Jesus and we praise you for the greatness of your love. Guide us during these final days of Advent, that the revelation of your love may be seen by others in us, in Jesus' name. Amen.

The Service for Christmas Eve or Christmas Day

CELEBRATION

The Opening Words (by leader)

Our hearts are filled with joy as we celebrate the birth of our Savior in Bethlehem's manger. We sing praises to God and glorify his name as the angels did on the night of his birth. We rejoice in the fact that the promise of long ago has now been fulfilled.

The Reading of the Lectionary Text

(Gospel suggested)

The Lighting of the Candles in the Advent Wreath

(As the first four candles are relighted and as the Christ candle is lighted, the leader may say:)

Today we relight the four candles in our Advent Wreath, reminding us of the expectation, preparation, proclamation and revelation of his coming. Now, as we light the Christ candle, we rejoice that the promise of God has been fulfilled in the coming of the Babe in Bethlehem's manger.

The Hymn: "Joy to the World, the Lord Is Come"

The Prayer (by leader)

O God, we celebrate your goodness to us as we join in the triumph and joy of Christmas. As your love has been revealed in all of its fullness, we pray that love may abound in our hearts during this special day. Grant that the spirit of the Christ-Child may dominate our lives in every way, as in his name we pray. Amen.

RESOURCES

An Advent Covenant Wreath by Douglas R. Behm, C.S.S. Publishing Company, Lima, Ohio, 1981.

Advent by Trudy Vander Haar, United Church Press, New York, New York, 1977.

The Jesse Tree by Raymond and Georgene Anderson, Fortress Press, Philadelphia, Pennsylvania, 1966.

The Jesse Tree, Sermons and Symbols for Advent by Donald R. Brewer, C.S.S. Publishing Company, Lima, Ohio, 1976.

Teaching and Celebrating Advent by Donald and Patricia Griggs, Abingdon Press, Nashville, Tennessee, 1970.

The Story of the Advent Wreath, Fortress Press, Philadelphia, Pennsylvania, 1982.

Advent materials in:
Lectionary Worship Aids, Series A
Lectionary Worship Aids, Series B
Lectionary Worship Aids, Series C
by Heth H. Corl, C.S.S. Publishing Company, Lima, Ohio, 1976, 1977, 1978.